the Brooks
WINCHESTER

THE FIRST YEAR OF THE EXCAVATION

WINCHESTER CITY COUNCIL & CULTURAL RESOURCE MANAGEMENT

2000 YEARS OF HISTORY

Each generation has left physical remnants of its presence in Winchester and many of these are now buried beneath more recent buildings. Every time the ground is disturbed an opportunity to learn more about the history of Winchester is created.

The City defences, first built by the Romans, remained largely intact until the 19th century, concentrating settlement in the same small area for nearly 2000 years. Founded soon after the invasion of AD 43, Winchester was to become the fifth largest town in Roman Britain. In Saxon times King Alfred made Winchester the first capital of England. The City prospered in the medieval period with many of its 8000 population engaged in the thriving wool and cloth industries.

The Brooks excavation is the largest single dig that Winchester has seen in 25 years of scientific archaeological research. This huge project is being undertaken because a major new shopping complex is to be built, which will lead to the total destruction of Roman, Saxon and medieval remains. The Archaeology Section of Winchester City Council has been given 17 months to investigate the site before building begins in August 1988.

The site lies right in the heart of the City, in an area known as the Brooks since the 16th century. The name is derived from the ancient watercourses that now flow beneath the three modern streets, Lower, Middle and Upper Brook Street. Within recent memory the site was covered with 19th century terraced housing but this was demolished to make way for the City's Central Car Park in the 1950s.

Enough information had been pieced together before the dig began to predict that the Central Car Park, or the Brooks, would be a unique site. Along its southern edge, bordering St George's Street, a Roman town house was discovered during excavations for Winchester City Museum in advance of a road widening scheme during 1953.

Further Roman remains were recognised in 1978 in a trial trench dug some 40m to the north. In both cases, the

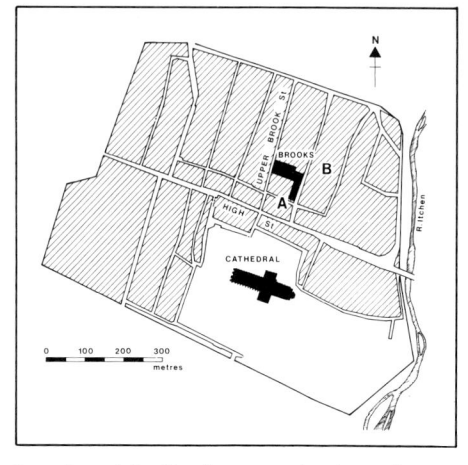

Location of the Brooks excavation in modern Winchester showing A) St George's Street site, 1953-54; B) Lower Brook Street site.

Roman layers dating back to the 1st century AD were much more accessible than usual in Winchester. For reasons still not fully understood they were not so deeply buried as usual and the overlying medieval remains had largely been removed.

In contrast, at the other end of the car park, another trial trench revealed that the medieval layers survived virtually undamaged by later activity. This discovery was greeted with great excitement because the medieval documents for the Brooks indicated that a prominent merchant's house once stood on the site facing Upper Brook Street.

This building had been the home of wealthy wool merchant and financier, John de Tytynge, a man chosen to represent Winchester in two of Edward I's parliaments and to serve as the City's mayor in 1299 and 1305. The massive area available for excavation would allow investigation of an entire, high status property, an opportunity that very rarely arises in medieval urban archaeology.

Documents also suggested that smaller properties, more typical of the Brooks in medieval times, would be found at the same end of the car park, but facing Middle Brook Street.

THE ROMAN TOWN

The earliest history of Roman Winchester is still far from clear. Finds from the first few years after the Roman conquest of AD 43 are still comparatively rare. The town was named *Venta Belgarum* – the market place of the Belgae people – but its relationship to the earlier Iron Age settlement is uncertain.

Many early Roman towns began life around a fort, but there is no conclusive evidence that this was the case in Winchester. A ditch of military character was found on the Lower Brook Street excavation in the 1960s and it is hoped that further evidence will be found on the Brooks dig during 1988.

Winchester's first town defences were built in about AD 75, not long before the street system was established. Unlike the modern street layout, which dates back to the time of King Alfred, the Roman streets formed a gridiron pattern with one or two slight irregularities. The blocks of land between the roads were

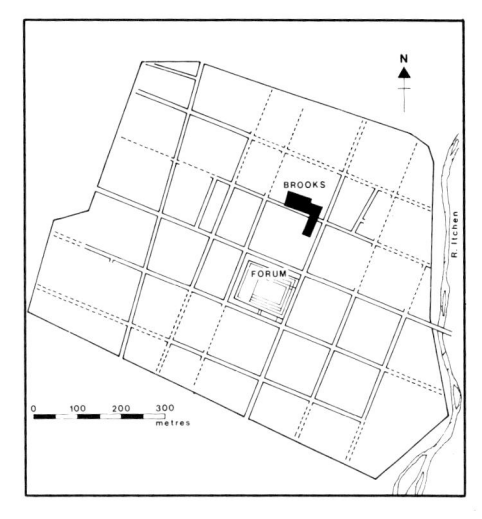

Plan of Roman Winchester showing the streets inside the city walls.

known as *insulae*, and the Brooks site lies on the *insula* immediately to the north of the *forum* and *basilica*, the commercial and administrative centre of the town. Traces of these public buildings were recognised during excavations in the 1960s in the area between the Cathedral and the modern High Street, and most recently in Market Street.

One important result of the Brooks excavation has been the confirmation of the precise line of an east-west gravel street that ran parallel to the Roman high street (today's High Street lies somewhat to the north of its Roman predecessor). The two were linked by a third street that was discovered beneath Middle Brook Street in 1953.

Although little is known about early Roman Winchester, rather more has been learned of its later history. During the late 3rd and early 4th centuries the town was a thriving, regional centre. The busy streets were lined with shops and houses built of masonry, their foundations having been discovered beneath Wolvesey Palace, Lower Brook Street, St George's Street, the High Street and now on the Brooks.

Wooden statuette of the goddess Epona found in a 2nd century pit at Lower Brook Street. Copyright Winchester Excavations Committee.

Artist's reconstruction of the Brooks area in the later Roman period with the forum and bascilica in the background. The excavated buildings are shown in colour: the Brooks town house is at the bottom left.

Many people would have lived above their places of work, two-storey buildings being a Roman innovation. These houses were usually long and narrow with the gable end facing onto the street. The Brooks houses, however, were larger buildings, in which the rooms were arranged around a central courtyard. This was because they were built by wealthier people following a fashion derived from the Mediterranean. Being so close to the High Street and the town's *forum,* the Brooks would have been a highly desirable residential area.

None of the courtyard houses discovered so far had private bathrooms attached to them, as it was probably only the very wealthy that could afford to indulge in this later Roman fashion. The inhabitants of the Brooks houses would have used the public baths, which have yet to be located.

In a town the size of Winchester there would have been a number of public temples, dedicated to various gods. Only one has been discovered so far, excavated in the 1960s at Lower Brook Street, a short distance from the present dig.

During the Roman period town dwellers were not allowed to bury their dead around their places of worship. Instead, their cemeteries had to be located outside the defended area and usually lined the roads leaving the town. More than 1400 burials, mostly of late-Roman date, have so far been found outside the walls of *Venta Belgarum.*

A great deal of archaeological investigation has taken place in Winchester over the last 35 years, and yet many mysteries still surround the Roman town in particular. Much research needs to be done if our knowledge of *Venta Belgarum* is to reach the level of understanding already achieved for many Romano-British towns.

South wall of the Brooks town house during excavation.

The Fourth-Century House

As a surface of the car park and the underlying 18th and 19th century remains were stripped back by machine in March 1987, the foundations of two Roman town houses began to appear. By the end of the summer careful excavation had revealed much of the story of these ancient buildings.

The first house, at the southern end of the site, now lies mostly under St George's Street. When the street was widened in 1953, it was possible to make out the plan of a range of rooms which are now covered by the road. They were linked by a corridor floored with an attractive red and white tessellated floor, that is, one made of coarse cubes of fired clay, stone or chalk, known as *tesserae*.

Virtually the entire ground plan of the second Roman town house fell within the Brooks excavation and, once again, was arranged around a central courtyard. It had been built in a prime location, right on the corner of a town centre *insula* overlooking two streets. The bases of most of the flint and mortar walls and some of the floors survived, including fragments of three mosaics. Some rooms had been damaged by rubbish pits dug during the medieval period long after the remains had disappeared from view.

The crudely cobbled courtyard was flanked by corridors on its northern and western sides. These were surfaced with plain red tessellated floors, except for a

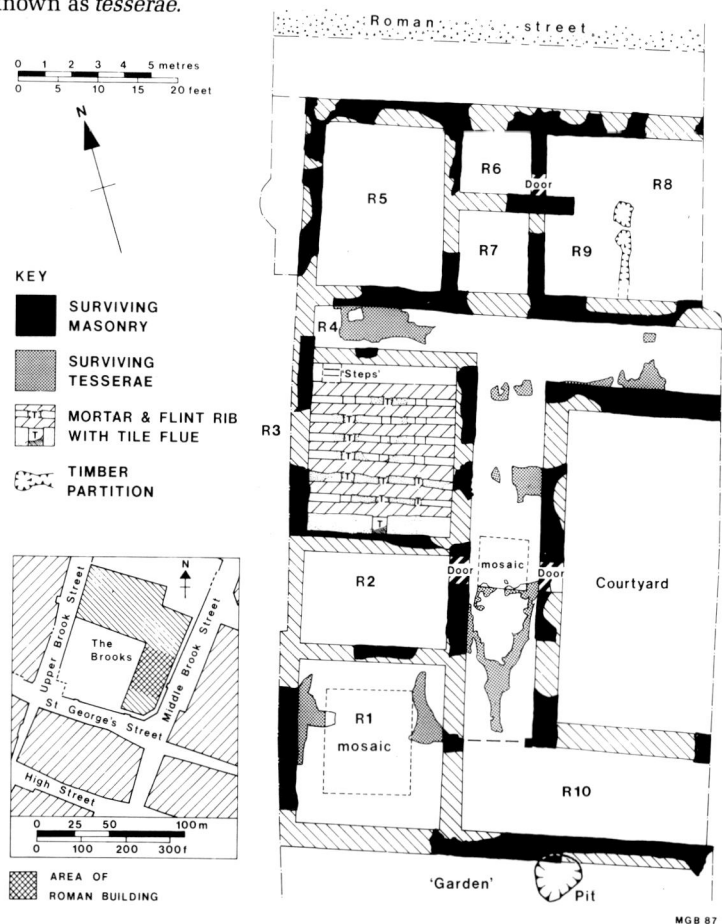

KEY
- SURVIVING MASONRY
- SURVIVING TESSERAE
- MORTAR & FLINT RIB WITH TILE FLUE
- TIMBER PARTITION

AREA OF ROMAN BUILDING

Plan of the Brooks town house.

2m square halfway along the western corridor.

This square had been filled with a mosaic panel with a geometric design but, sadly, it had been badly crushed at some stage and then disturbed after the building was abandoned. Enough did survive, however, to show that its outer border was made of alternate red and black triangles separated by white lines. The contrasting colours were provided by tiny cubes chipped from clay tiles and various types of stone.

The mosaic marked the point of access from the central courtyard into the western range of rooms. This was once the residential wing of the house, while the northern range of rooms probably included the service rooms, such as the kitchen and pantries.

Two out of the four rooms in the residential wing had once been decorated with mosaic floors, one of which rested on an underfloor heating system or *hypocaust*. The mosaic fragment surviving in Room 1 had a geometric design, incorporating lozenge shapes outlined in red, white and black. It formed the centrepiece of the room, framed by the coarser red *tesserae* like those used to surface the corridors. The surface of the mosaic was discoloured as if scorched by a charcoal brazier used to heat the room.

Room 3 must have been the finest room of the house with its mosaic floor and heating system. Only a tiny fragment of the mosaic survived but it was of rather better quality than the other two mosaics and had been carefully grouted with cement.

The room was heated by a furnace built into the outer wall of the building. Hot air travelled under the floor, up flues built into the walls and was drawn out through openings in the roof.

In most *hypocaust* systems, stacks of tiles supported the floor to allow free circulation of hot air, but here there were parallel flint and mortar walls about 40cm (1 foot 4 inches) apart. Openings lined with tiles were left along their length at intervals of about 1m (3 foot 3 inches) to allow the air to pass from one channel to another. A section of one of the flues, consisting of three box-shaped tiles, survived in the eastern wall of the room.

The 'lozenge' mosaic in Room 1.

Reconstruction of the 'lozenge' mosaic (D. E. Johnston).

The walls of this room, and others in the residential wing, would have been covered with brightly painted plaster, remnants of which were found along the bottom of a wall in the western corridor. Courtyard houses were usually single storey buildings with either tiled or stone roofs. Those found at the Brooks were roofed using lozenge-shaped pieces of limestone brought from Purbeck in Dorset.

Judging from its moderate size (20m × 27m) and the quality of the internal decoration, the Brooks Roman house falls at the budget end of the provincial town house market! It was perhaps built by someone of Decurion status (a member of the town council), but not an individual of great wealth.

The house might well have stood for nearly 100 years, but was finally demolished in the 4th century. Unusually, most of the building materials were immediately removed from the site.

At about the same time, a pit was dug up against the south wall of the house. A fascinating array of objects was uncovered when it was excavated. This included over 100 beads made of green, white and blue glass, of amber, coral and ivory and with a tiny bronze clasp, possibly from a two-string necklace.

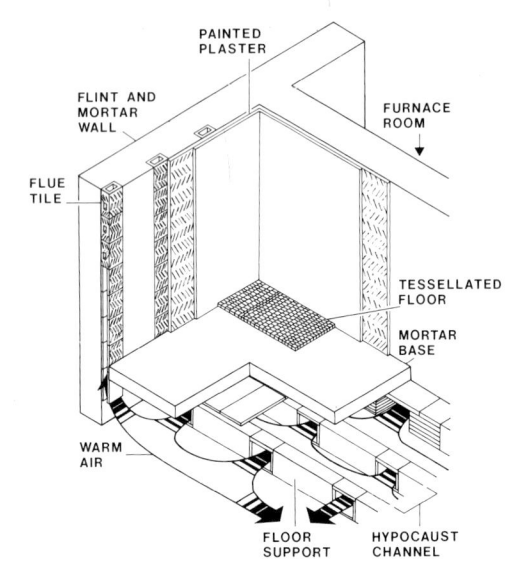

Cutaway view showing channelled hypocaust in operation.

There were also about 50 coins, many of which were minims – tiny local copies of official late Roman coins. It seems likely that they were put in a container and deliberately buried, but it is not clear whether the building was still standing or in ruins at the time.

Remains of hypocaust channels in Room 3.

Beads, probably from a late Roman necklace, found in a pit outside the town house.

THE DARK AGES

After the Roman houses had been demolished the site became overgrown, and a thick layer of soil gradually formed. The ruins disappeared from view for over 1600 years.

This sequence of events is similar to that known from earlier excavations in the City. Demolition of town houses is found to occur at a time when the defences were strengthened by the addition of external towers or bastions. Winchester may have changed from a thriving market town into an industrial centre, possibly with a military garrison. Only further excavation will be able to cast light on this poorly understood period of history.

There is little evidence for the fate of the town after the withdrawal of the Roman legions from Britain early in the 5th century. Excavations near the site of the *forum* revealed that houses were built over the Roman streets soon after Roman authority was removed. Otherwise, little evidence of occupation exists within the walled area until the 7th century.

Anglo-Saxon disc brooch found in a cemetery near Winchester.

REBIRTH OF A TOWN

In comparison to the earlier periods, a wealth of information exists for late Saxon and medieval Winchester. Intensive documentary research and widespread archaeological investigation have revealed that Winchester re-emerged as an urban centre in Saxon times over 1000 years ago.

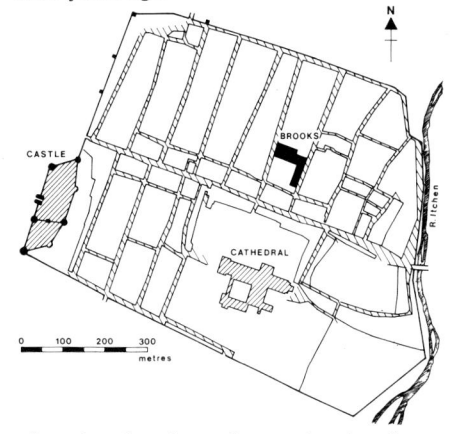

Plan of medieval Winchester, showing the streets inside the city walls.

Having selected Winchester as his capital, King Alfred rebuilt the crumbling Roman defences and established the street system which is still in use today. One of England's greatest royal and religious centres, Winchester reached the height of its prosperity by the 12th century but had already begun to lose its pre-eminence as a royal centre to London. Within 200 years, at the time of the Black Death, royal links with the City had further weakened, and its economy had gone into decline.

Throughout this period, the Brooks area of Winchester played a vital role. The streams that ran down Upper, Middle and Lower Brooks Street attracted industries that needed a reliable water supply, such as cloth and leather processing. The families whose livelihoods depended on these industries had their houses amongst the workshops and storehouses. The homes of two of these families were excavated during the first year of the Brooks excavation.

A Saxon king and courtiers.

Artist's reconstruction of the excavated medieval building at the Brooks, with the merchant's house in the foreground.

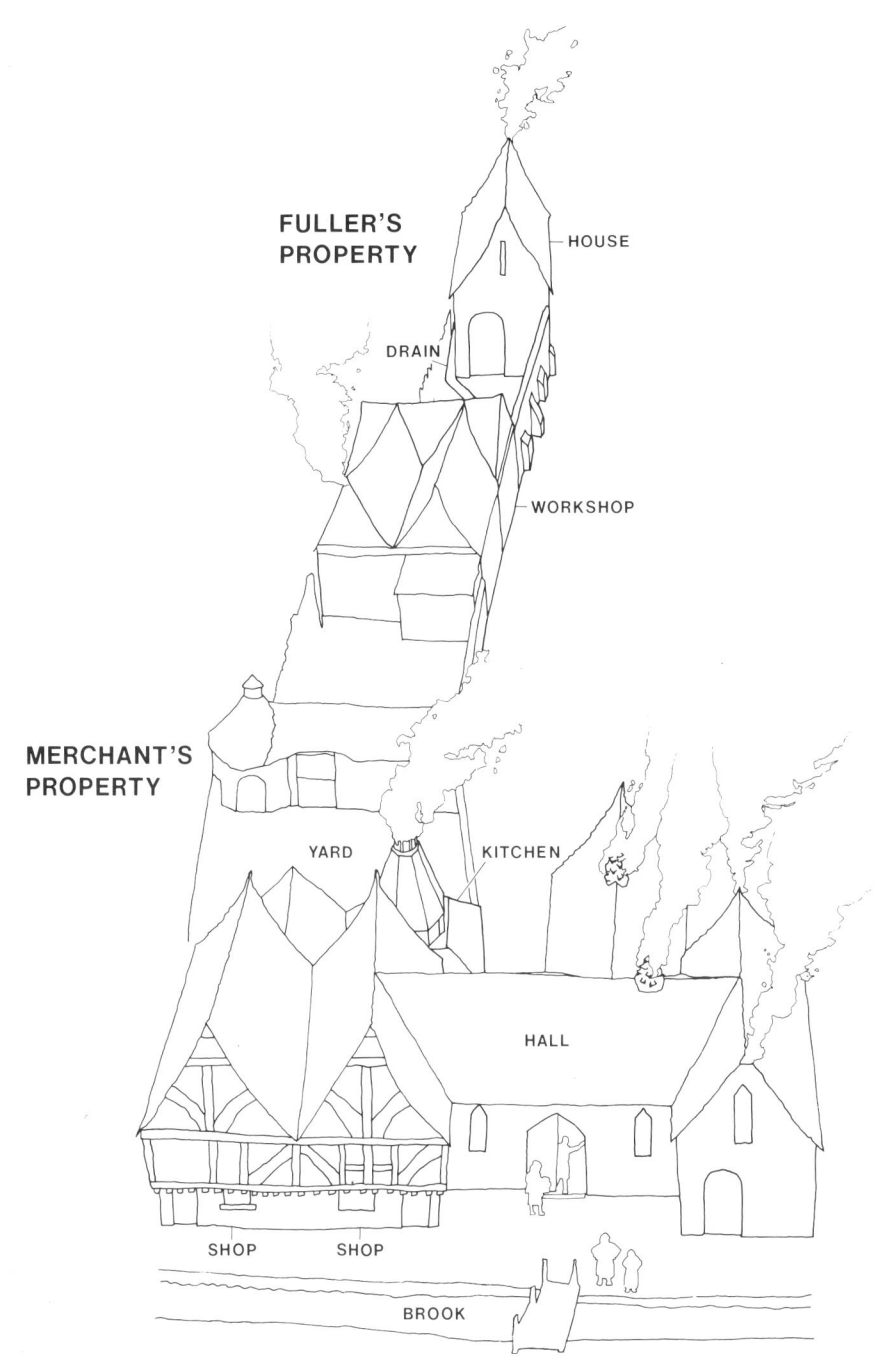

Key to the drawing opposite.

The Merchant's House

Research into the City's surviving medieval documents has enabled historians to pin-point the location of the properties occupied by Winchester's leading merchants. An extensive plot on Upper Brook Street was the home of wealthy merchant and financier John de Tytynge in the late 13th century. The documents report that it had a 'great gate' of more than 100 feet (30.8m) on its frontage, surely a house of massive proportions.

This entire property was thought to fall within the area of the Central Car Park to be redeveloped. Trial investigation showed that relatively little modern disturbance had affected the site. Medieval experts are very rarely given the opportunity to totally excavate a high status residence of this kind. It was certainly the first chance to do so in Winchester.

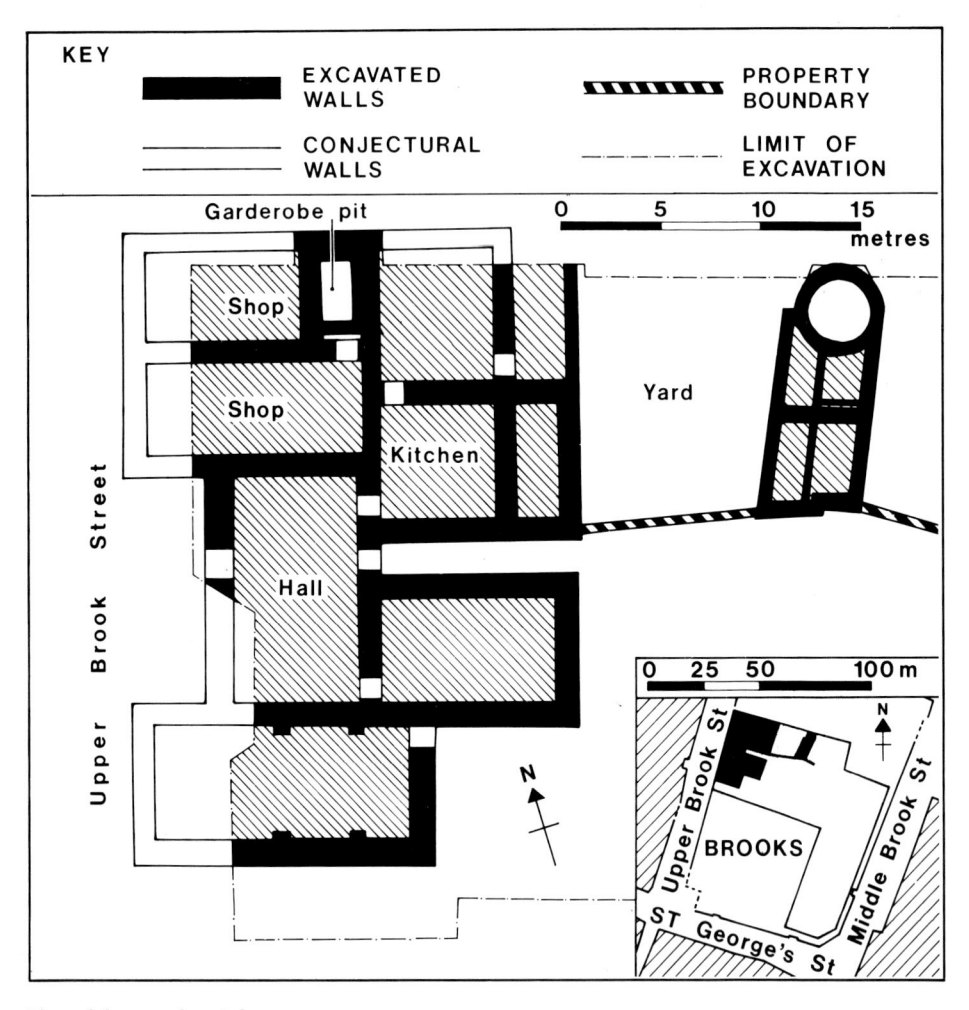

Plan of the merchant's house.

By the end of the summer of 1987 the complete ground plan of the house had been exposed, apart from the front wall which lay beneath Upper Brook Street. This street dates to Saxon times but has been resurfaced many times over the centuries, and recent widenings have buried the front 4m (13 feet) of the house.

Gradually the relative ages of the various wall foundations and floors have been worked out and the story of the building has begun to unfold. Three stages of development have been recognised. Before John de Tytynge's time there had been two separate buildings on the site, a domestic, one-roomed building open to the roof, called a hall, to the south, and two shops with a hall behind to the north. They were divided by a narrow, gravel lane that ran back from Upper Brook Street.

By the 14th century, however, the two buildings had been linked together and extended to create the great merchant's house described in the contemporary documents. Most of the new building provided more private accommodation, a new two-storey wing to the south and new chambers above the shops. This work may well have been commissioned by John de Tytynge.

The centrepiece was a new hall built parallel to the street and across the earlier gravel lane. This large room was dominated by opposing doors about 2.60m (8 feet 6 inches) wide. The path between them was lightly gravelled and followed the line of the old lane – it must have remained the main route into the back yards. Perhaps this was the 'great gate' referred to in the documents.

All the adjoining rooms could be reached from the hall, but the route between the main entrance and what must have been the kitchen was particularly heavily worn. This well-used room contained the remains of several hearths and ovens arranged along one wall. The chalk and mortar floor had been repaired time and time again. Each new floor layer trapped thick deposits of ash, and traces of medieval meals in the form of seeds and small animal bones were preserved.

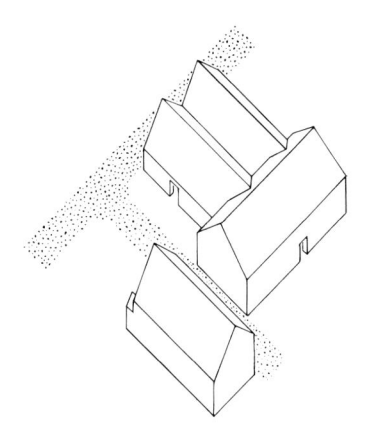

PHASE A 12-13th cent.

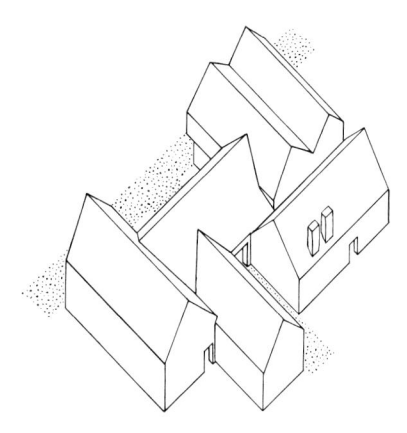

PHASE B c.1300

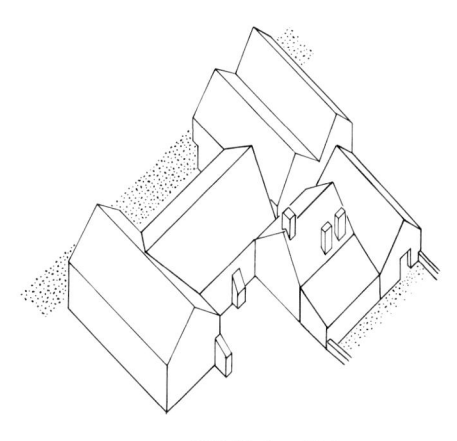

PHASE C c.1352

The development of the merchant's house (G. Scobie).

Aerial view of the merchant's house. Upper Brook Street lies to the right of the picture.

The function of one of the other new rooms was easier to identify than most! This was a small room almost filled by a large, rectangular garderobe, or indoor latrine pit. It had been inserted into the back of one of the shops incorporated into the enlarged merchant's house. About 1.40m (4 foot 6 inches) deep, the pit was carefully lined with chalk blocks but rested on an earthen base.

There was, however, no known access to the pit on the ground floor so this must have been provided on the first floor in the new private rooms above the shops. The sewage probably reached the pit down a chute on one side of the room.

The last stage in the life of this property was marked by the sub-division of John de Tytynge's old house in about 1350.

The southern property, which embraced the great hall or gate, was allowed to fall into disrepair and was virtually rebuilt by the new owner, Hugh le Cran, citizen and draper.

The occupants of the northern property, which incorporated the garderobe, reorganised the kitchens and extended the outbuildings. These included a large, circular dovecote, which would actually have housed pigeons, a valuable, year round, source of fresh meat.

The garderobe in the merchant's house, showing timbers and possible toilet seat collapsed into the pit.

Two decorated jugs and a cup, imported from Saintonge in southern France, found in the garderobe pit.

The contents of the garderobe, probably belonging to the last occupation of the house in the late 14th century, have provided more insights into medieval life at the Brooks than any other aspect of the site. A small sample has been analysed and found to hold masses of information on the diet and general health of the household.

The food remains, those of a well-to-do family, included cultivated and imported fruit, such as fig and grapes with sloe probably being the only wild species present. As well as the more durable eel, fish and bird bones, there were large quantities of cereals and plant tissue from leeks and onions. Even the herbs and spices used to flavour these foods survived, including coriander, caraway, parsley and dill.

Despite their rich and varied diet those using the garderobe suffered from parasites such as whipworm and large roundworm. Just 50 years after this period of use, both buildings had been demolished and the site left open. Some of the building debris found its way into the latrine pit, as well as a wooden privy seat and a fine collection of rather more exotic artefacts. Coming from countries such as France and Spain, they represent the many links established by Winchester merchants across medieval Europe.

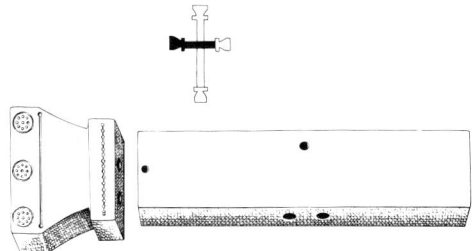

Part of a worked and polished jet cross with silver inlay, found in the garderobe pit. It was probably a Spanish import (D. Cunliffe).

The Fuller's House

The fuller's property, located to the east of the merchant's house, along Middle Brook Street, would have had far more in common with the majority of properties in medieval Winchester than that of the wealthy John de Tytynge.

It was built at right angles to Middle Brook Street on a thin strip of land about 9m wide (29 feet) which stretched back nearly 40m (130 feet). Along the city centre streets, such as this one, plots of land were often very narrow so that the maximum number of properties could benefit from a street frontage.

The earliest building on the street frontage dates to the mid-12th century and was possibly that of Roger, the vintner (wine merchant) who rented the property from the King in 1148.

The house had a cellar built largely out of skilfully-cut chalk blocks fitted with great precision. The cellar floor was about 1m (3 feet 3 inches) below the level of the back yard. The cellar would certainly have made an excellent wine store.

In the 13th century, for reasons unknown, the upper part of Roger's cellar and the hall above it were demolished and replaced by the fuller's house. The side walls were built on top of their predecessors but the back wall was angled away from the original line and had to be supported on timber piles. The corner of the building not resting on the earlier cellar was further strengthened by three small relieving arches that effectively redistributed the building's weight onto the adjacent walls.

Compared to the earlier cellar, these 13th century walls were crudely built, of coarse chalk rubble, flints and mortar. The structure was, however, roofed with small, grey slates and colourful glazed tiles.

Across the gravelled back yard behind the fuller's house was the workshop which gave the property its name. It was possibly associated with John Newman, fuller and citizen, who held the property in 1417. This rectangular building housed a stone tank about 1.80m (5 feet 10 inches) by 1.30m (4 feet 3 inches), that emptied into an open, chalk-lined drain. This crossed the yard into the Middle Brook, now culverted beneath the modern street.

View of the fuller's property, with the back wall of the house in the foreground and the yard and workshop beyond. Middle Brook Street is at the bottom of the picture; north is to the right.

The tank was used for fulling, a cloth finishing process that involves washing and treading cloth underfoot to create a denser, more hard-wearing fabric. A thin mineral deposit of fuller's earth was found in the tank. When wet, fuller's earth has a soapy feel and acts as a detergent to remove excess oils and dirt.

The floor inside the workshop was made of thin layers of chalk and mortar, which trapped lenses of dirt in between them. Very few fragments of pottery or bone were discovered in the house or workshop, indicating that the floors were kept clean. The workshop floors, however, did provide evidence of how the room was subdivided. Stake-holes, small earth-filled holes left after the removal of wooden partitions, divided one half of the room into compartments perhaps used for storage of materials.

During the 13th or 14th centuries the workshop was extended at the back. The remaining section of the plot – largely garden – was enclosed by a boundary wall. Within 100 years, however, both house and extended workshop had been demolished and the entire property turned over to gardens.

Medieval cloth dyeing.

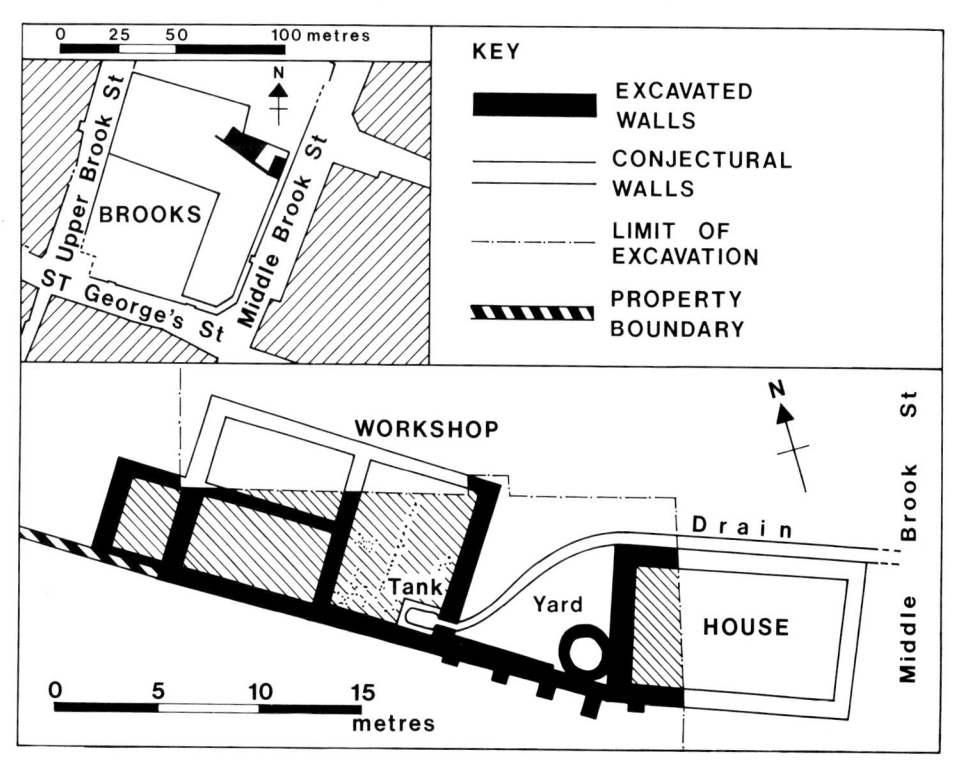

Plan of the fuller's house and workshop.

AFTER THE MIDDLE AGES

The Brooks excavation has uncovered little evidence of the 15th-17th centuries, and this may reflect the decline of Winchester during that time. There have been, however many discoveries that illustrate the revitalisation of the City in the 18th century.

The area became cluttered with small workshops and houses. Clay pipe makers, for example, began to concentrate around Middle Brook Street. Pipes found on the site can be identified by the makers' marks stamped on them. Debris from a kiln, amost certainly that of a mid-18th century pipe maker called John Marchant, has been found.

Pipe makers often set up their workshops close to public houses, as these were one of the main outlets for their product. Some unexpected archaeological evidence for these 18th century drinking haunts came up on the Brooks site. A disused well, presumably in the backyard of a pub, contained a remarkable collection of objects associated with drinking. Glass wine bottles, glasses, stamped clay pipes and, finest of all, a pair of large stoneware tankards in perfect condition were found.

The tankards were engraved with the names of 'R. Lamb' and 'Lashford', and one was dated 1745. The lists of licensed victuallers, or publicans, in the City of Winchester for the years around 1745 all include the names Richard Lamb and Daniel Lashford! What is more, a third tankard found elsewhere on the site was engraved with a chequerboard design, unremarkable but for the fact that Mr Lashford's inn was called The Chequers.

Eighteenth century street scene.

Eighteenth century stoneware beer tankards and glass wine bottles.

As the population of Winchester grew during the 19th century, the Brooks area became an increasingly cramped and unhygienic place to live. The three brooks continued to be used both as open sewers and sources of drinking water, until the latter half of the century.

Because of limits of time, many of the archaeological remains of this period, such as the foundations of terraced houses and workshops, were deliberately removed by machine to reveal the late medieval layers below.

An exception was the eight skeletons of horses found buried in shallow graves in the area of John de Tytynge's house, just off Upper Brook Street. There had been stables and a blacksmith's workshop on this site in the 19th century. The cause of death, and the reason for the horses' unusual burial place, have yet to be established. Research and analysis will be undertaken after the end of the excavation.

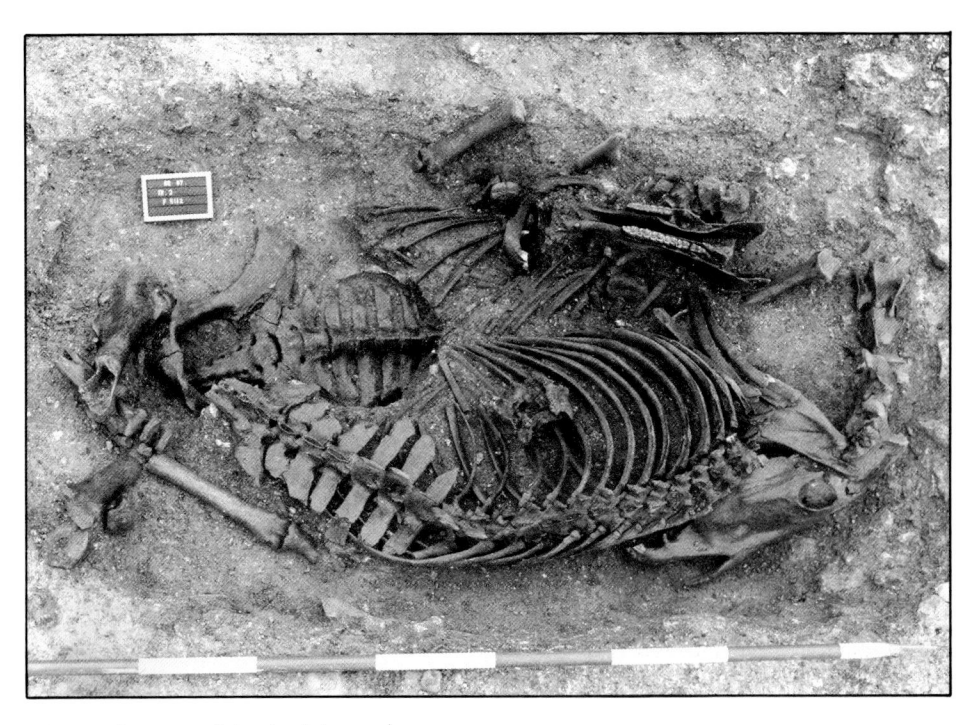

Nineteenth century horse burial.

WHAT NEXT?

In July 1988 the excavation of the Brooks will come to an end and construction of a shopping complex with undergroud car parking will begin. Some intriguing problems need to be solved before then.

The first concerns the very origins of Winchester. Every other major town of Roman Britain grew up around a fort or a native centre. The key to Winchester's early development has still not been found, though the discovery of possible military ditches at Lower Brook Street in 1971 suggests it may lie in the Brooks area. The discovery of a terret, a bronze ring once part of a horse harness, on the Brooks excavation strengthens this possibility, for such objects are often associated with Roman military presence.

A second problem still to be resolved is the function of the timber-lined pits discovered near the much earlier Roman town houses. They were dug at about the time of the Norman Conquest and may have been used for tanning, a foul-smelling process that converted animal hides into leather. It would be surprising if such an unpleasant industry was carried out so near to the town centre.

A final problem revolves around the medieval merchant's house. Virtually the entire building has been excavated but the story will not be complete until the back yards, stables and gardens have been examined. Here the household rubbish – pottery, animal bone, seeds, wood and leather is likely to be found. Information gleaned from these objects will give us a picture of life in a great merchant's house in the 14th century, and an insight into the economy, diet, trade, crafts and industry of the people of medieval Winchester.

Even if these problems can all be solved during the time allowed for excavation, the archaeologist's work will continue while construction takes place. Study and analysis of all the artefacts and records recovered from the Brooks will lead, eventually, to publication of the main results. The material will then be carefully stored, or put on display, by Winchester Museums Service.

Bronze terret, probably 1st century AD.

Artist's impression of the completed Brooks development (courtesy of Ladbroke City and County Land Co Ltd).

Within the new shopping complex appropriate decorative motifs and design ideas inspired by the excavation will be incorporated into the building finishes. A Brooks 'visitor trail' will lead by means of distinctive paving to a series of displays around the development, supported by an educational resource area. As a result, Winchester shoppers will be reminded of their City's colourful past for many years to come.